A Tiny Beak

and Spiky Feathers

Ruby Tuesday Books

Whose Little Baby Are You?

by Ellen Lawrence

Published in 2016 by Ruby Tuesday Books Ltd.

Editor: Mark J. Sachner
Designer: Emma Randall
Production: John Lingham
With thanks to Rebecca Fox,
Assistant Professor of Biology,
Transylvania University,
Lexington, Kentucky

Photo Credits:
Alamy: 8, 12, 17, 19; Cosmographics: 23; FLPA: 10–11,
18–19, 20–21; Shutterstock: Cover, 1, 4–5, 6–7, 9, 13,
14–15, 16, 22–23.

Library of Congress Control Number: 2015940231

ISBN 978-1-910549-24-7

Printed and published in the United States of America

For further information including rights and
permissions requests, please contact our Customer
Service Department at 877-337-8577.

Contents

Words shown in **bold** in the text are explained in the glossary.

A Tiny Chick

In the trunk of an old gum tree, there is a small hole.

Gum tree →

← Nest hole

The hole leads to a cozy nest.

Inside the nest, a tiny, fluffy chick has just **hatched** from its egg.

The baby bird cannot see, walk, or fly.

Chick

Fluffy feathers

Who does this little baby belong to?

The tiny chick belongs to a mother and father cockatiel.

Mother cockatiel

Egg

The mother cockatiel laid five eggs in the nest.

The parent birds take turns sitting on the eggs and keeping them warm.

Sometimes the father bird
stands guard outside the nest.

Father
cockatiel

Now a chick has hatched from one of the eggs.

The hungry chick begs his mom and dad for food.

A one-day-old cockatiel chick

Beak

8

The parent birds
eat seeds.

Then they spit up the
mushy seeds into
the chick's tiny beak.

Soon, the little chick is not alone.

His brothers and sisters hatch from their eggs, too.

A four-day-old chick

The hungry babies wait in the nest for their parents to bring them food.

A father cockatiel looking for seeds

Crest

A 10-day-old chick

Spikes

After 10 days, the chick's eyes are nearly open and his fluffy yellow feathers are falling out.

Growing from his body are tiny gray spikes that will become new feathers.

A little **crest** sprouts from his head.

He doesn't look much like his father, but he soon will!

Crest

Feathers

Father cockatiel

When the chick is 15 days old, he is nearly as big as his mom and dad.

Tiny feathers sprout from the spikes on his body.

He practices flapping his little wings.

A 15-day-old chick

Wing

Feathers

14

When the chick is four weeks old, he has feathers and can fly.

He leaves the nest to explore with his brothers and sisters.

A four-week-old chick

16

At eight weeks old, the chick looks just like a grown-up.

An eight-week-old chick

Father cockatiel

Now he is ready to leave his parents and take care of himself.

Cockatiels live in large groups called **flocks**.

The young bird lives in a flock with lots of other cockatiels.

By the time he is six months old, he has yellow feathers on his head.

A six-month-old cockatiel

19

When he is 18 months old, the cockatiel finds a **mate**.

Now he is ready to be a father.

Together, the pair of cockatiels will raise chicks of their own!

Male cockatiel

Female cockatiel

21

Fact File

All About Cockatiels

A cockatiel is a type of small parrot.

Many people raise cockatiels as pets.

Wild cockatiels eat seeds from grasses and other plants. They also eat berries.

An adult cockatiel weighs about 3 ounces (85 g).

This picture shows a life-size adult male cockatiel.

Where Do Cockatiels Live?

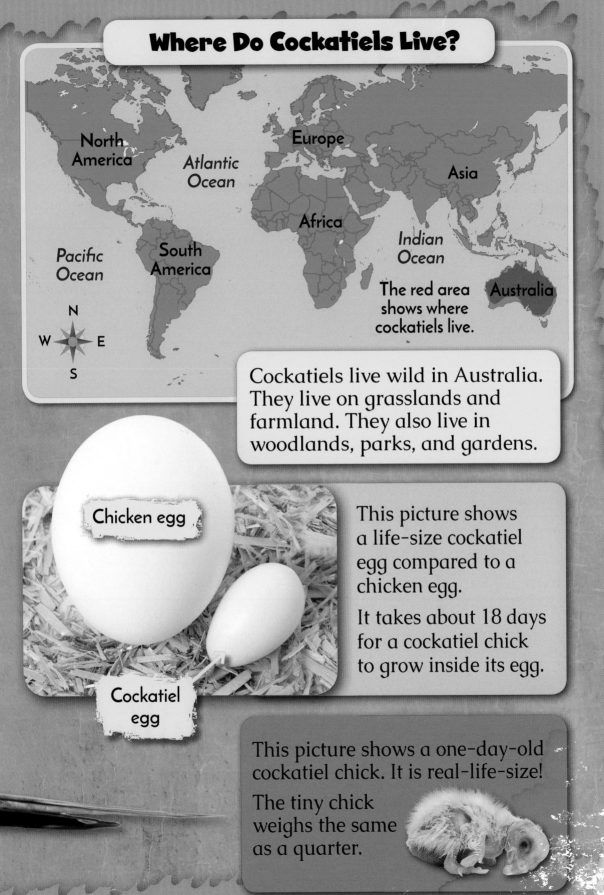

North America

Atlantic Ocean

Europe

Asia

Africa

Indian Ocean

Pacific Ocean

South America

The red area shows where cockatiels live.

Australia

N
W E
S

Cockatiels live wild in Australia. They live on grasslands and farmland. They also live in woodlands, parks, and gardens.

Chicken egg

Cockatiel egg

This picture shows a life-size cockatiel egg compared to a chicken egg.

It takes about 18 days for a cockatiel chick to grow inside its egg.

This picture shows a one-day-old cockatiel chick. It is real-life-size!

The tiny chick weighs the same as a quarter.

Glossary

crest (KREST)
A tuft of feathers, fur, or skin on the head of an animal.

flock (FLOK)
A large group of birds of the same kind that fly or live together.

hatched (HACHTD)
Broke out of an egg.

mate (MATE)
An animal's partner with which it has babies.

Index

Read More

Howard, Fran. *Parrots (First Facts)*. Mankato, MN: Capstone Press (2013).

Lawrence, Ellen. *A Bird's Life (Animal Diaries: Life Cycles)*. New York: Bearport Publishing (2013).

Learn More Online

To learn more about cockatiels, go to
www.rubytuesdaybooks.com/whoselittlebaby